LET'S FILL COLORS

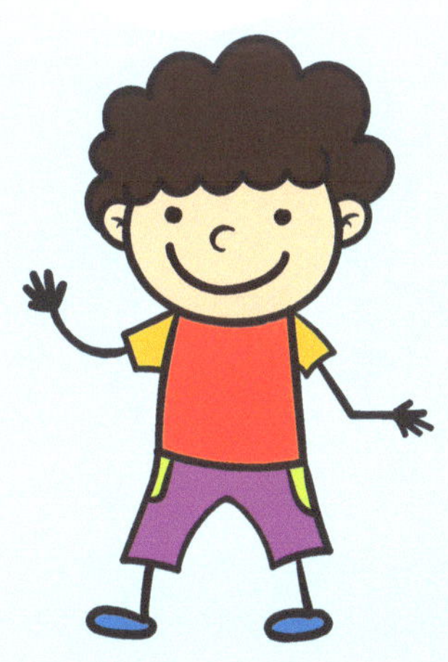

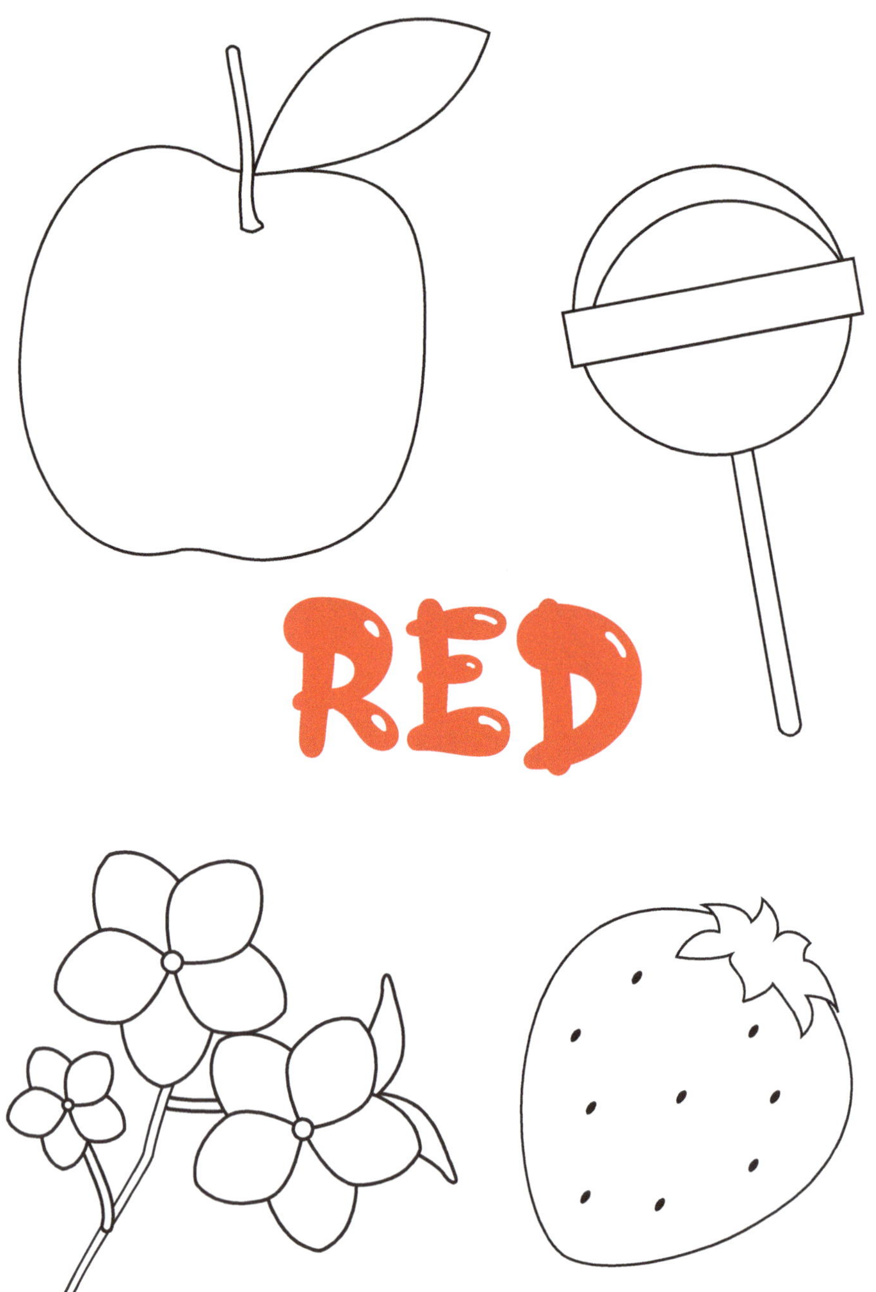
RED

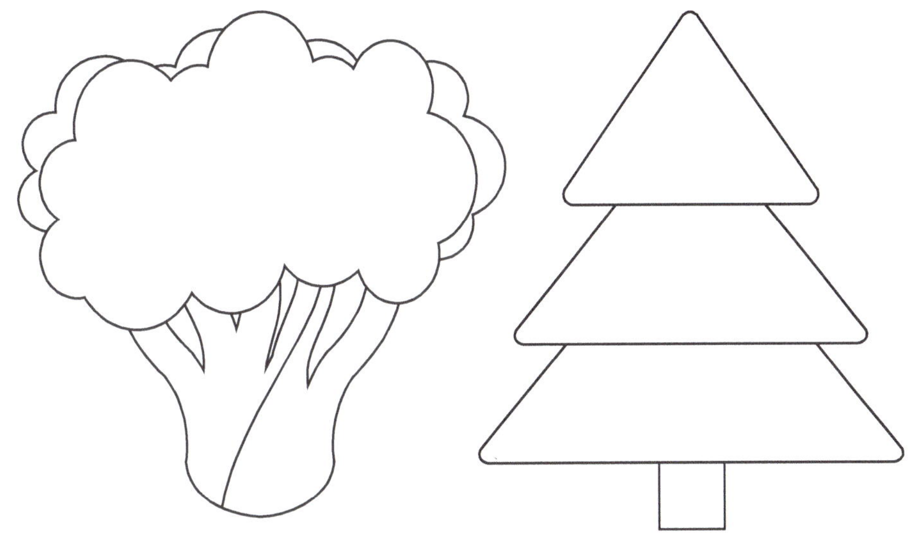

GREEN

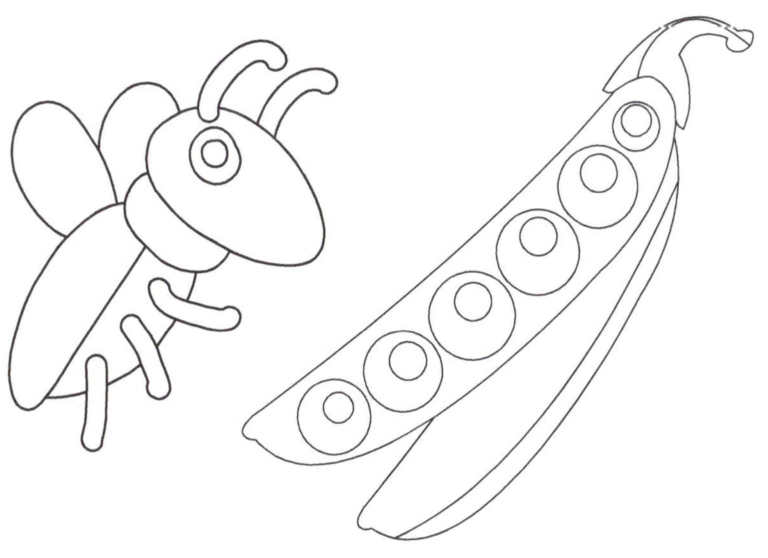

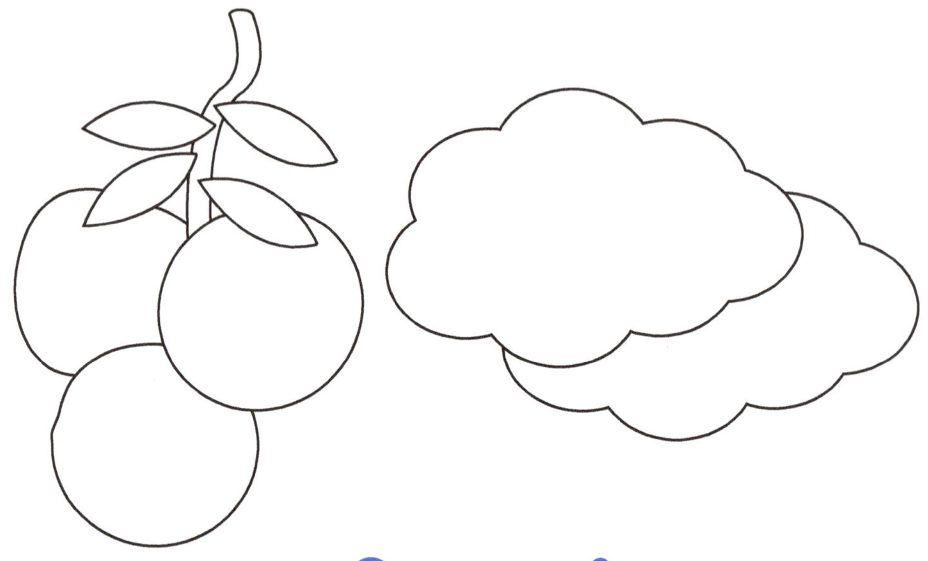

BLUE

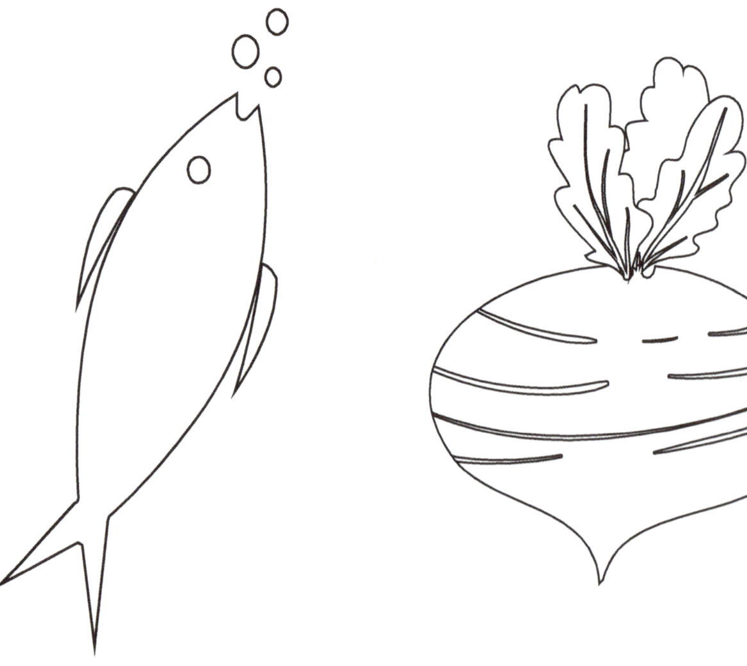

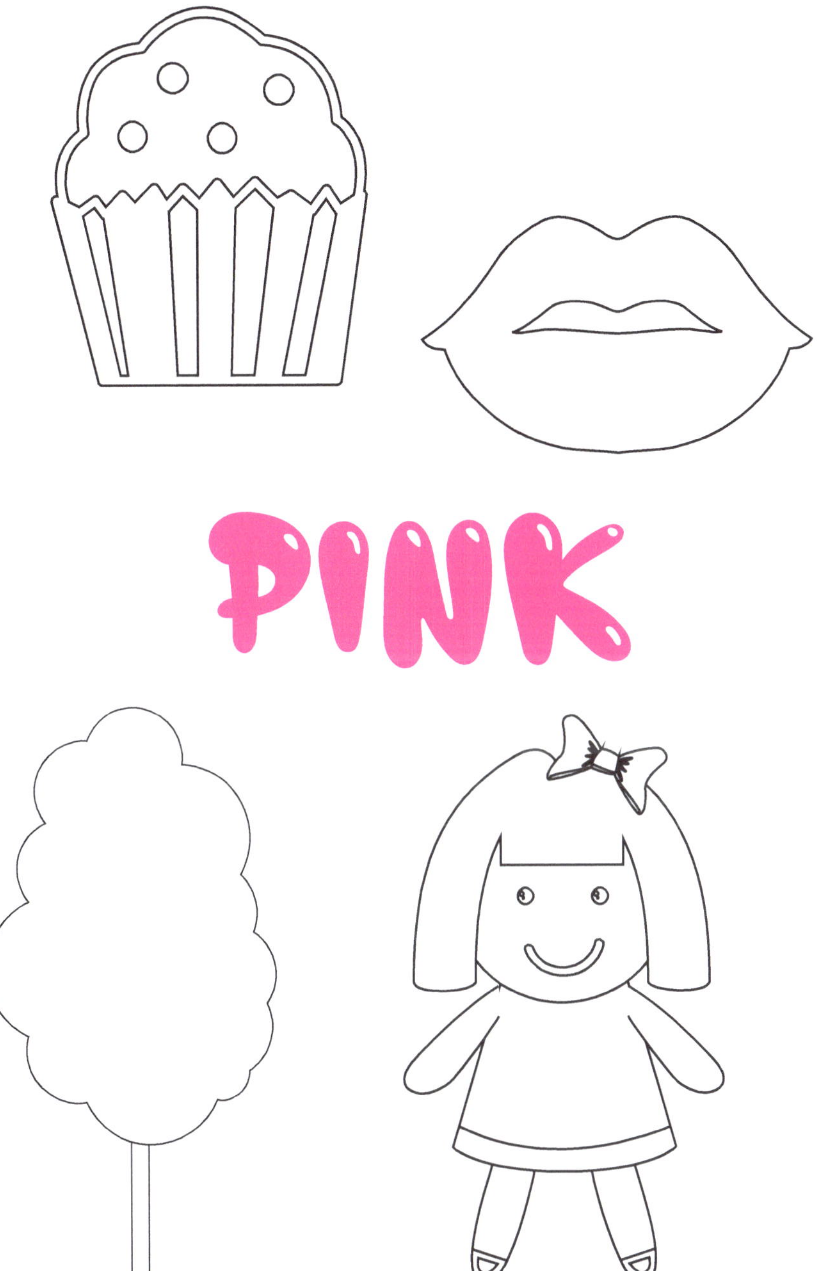

PINK

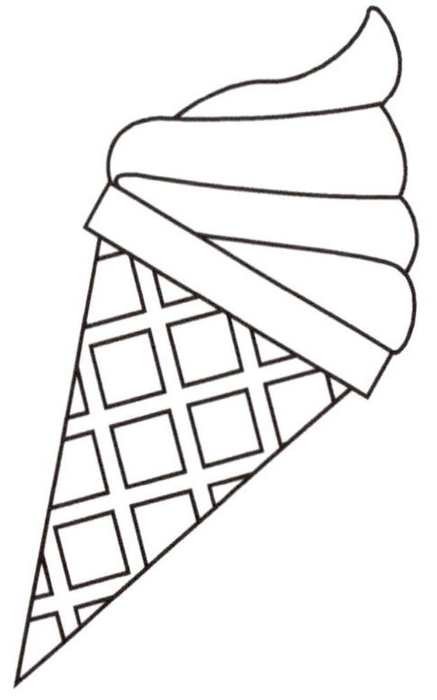
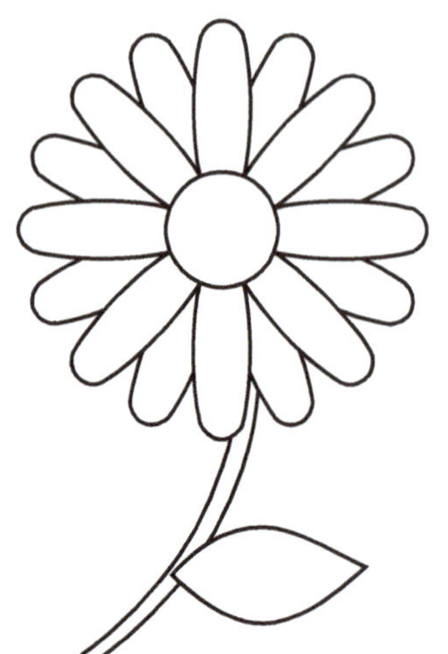

PURPLE

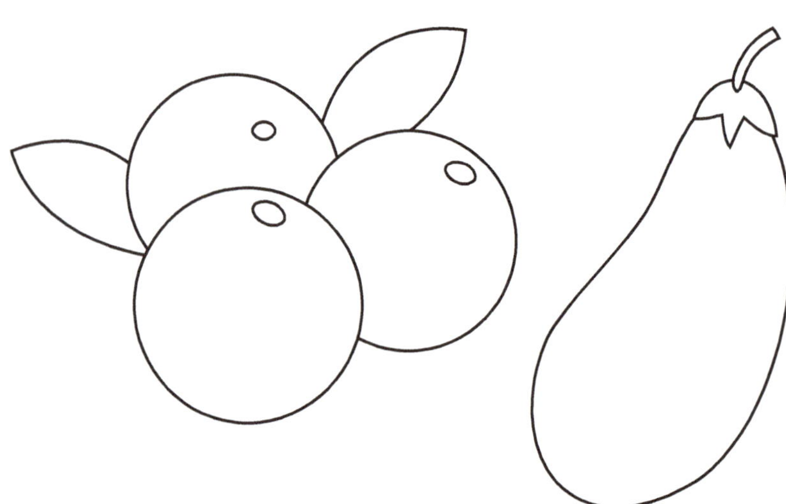

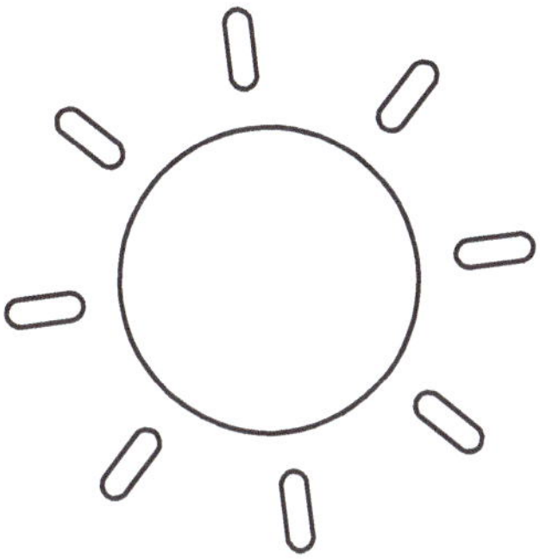

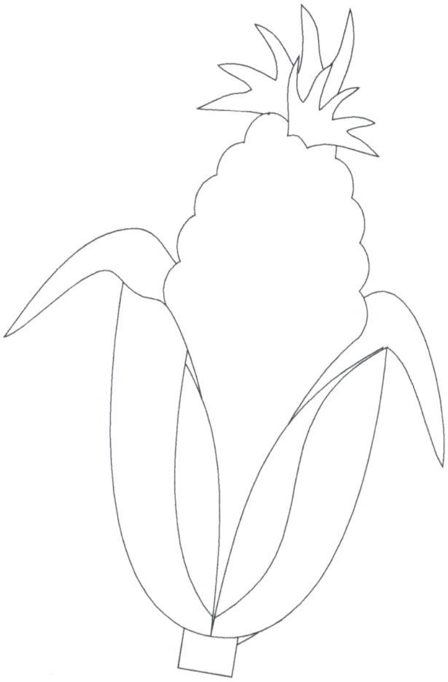

YELLOW

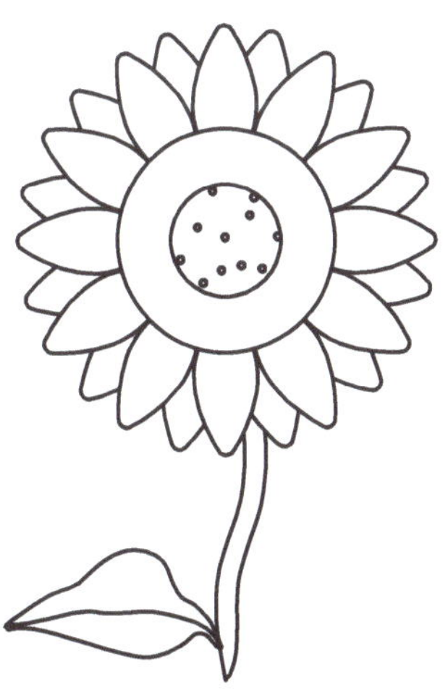

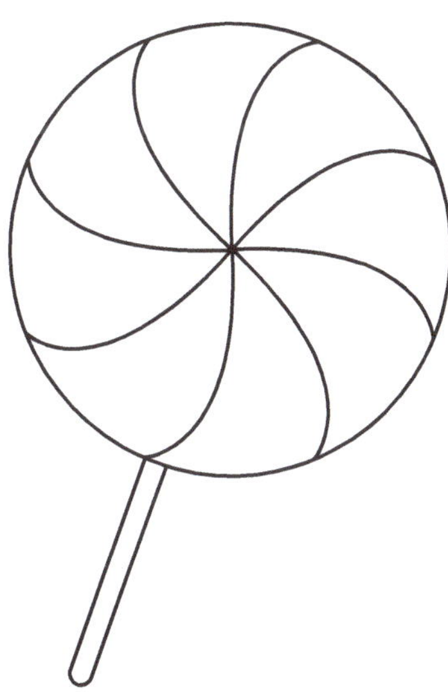

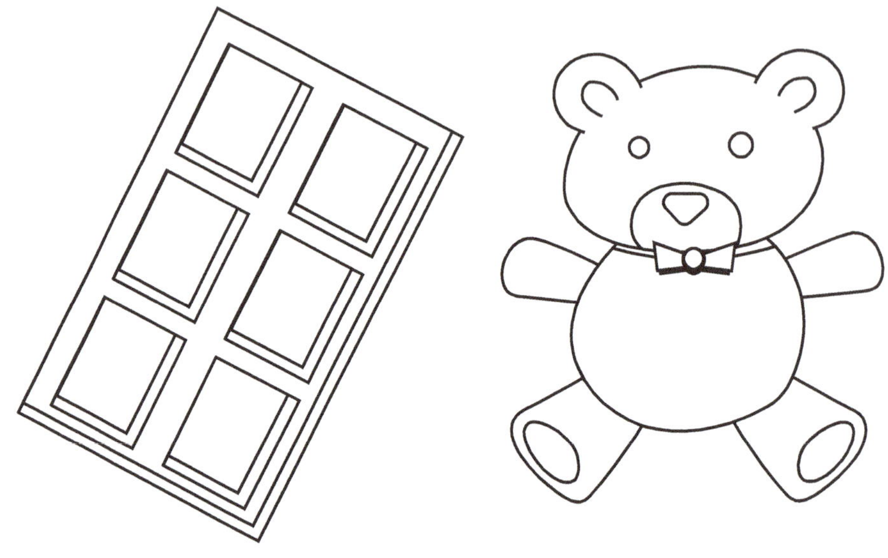

BROWN

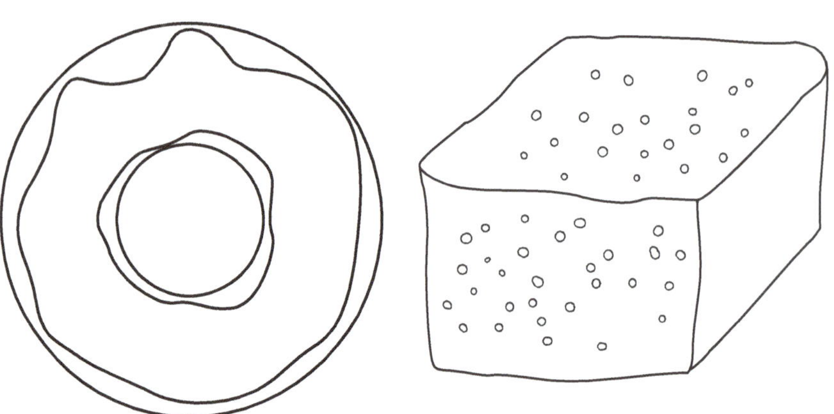

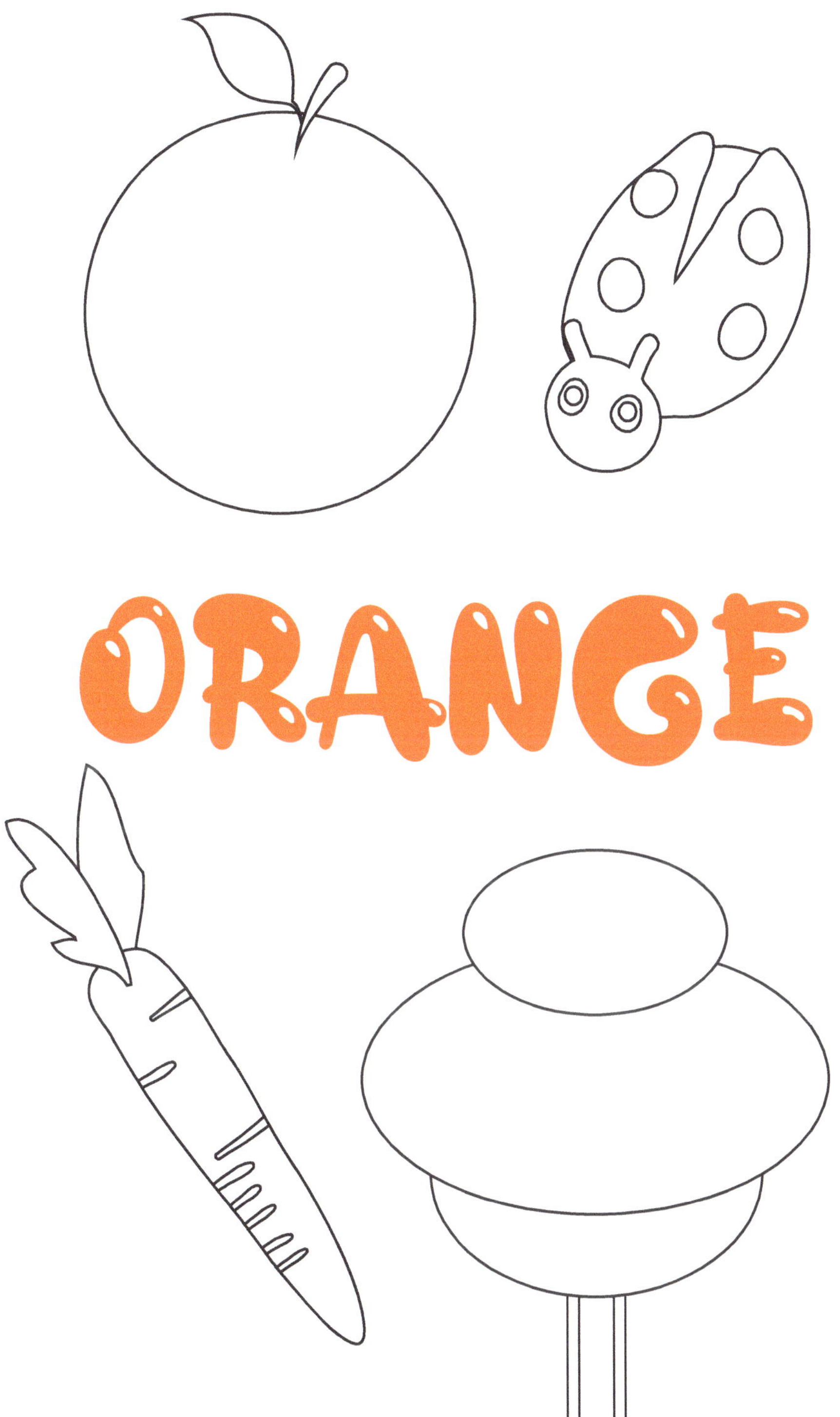

ORANGE

WHITE

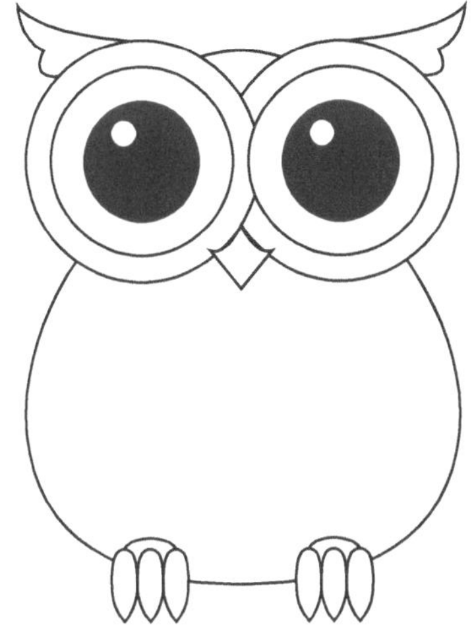

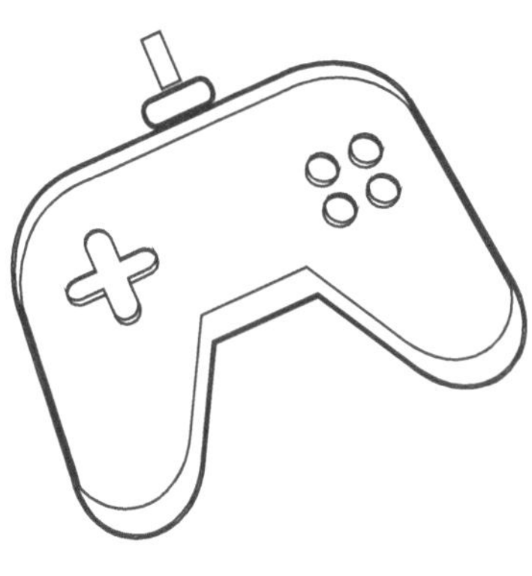

GREY

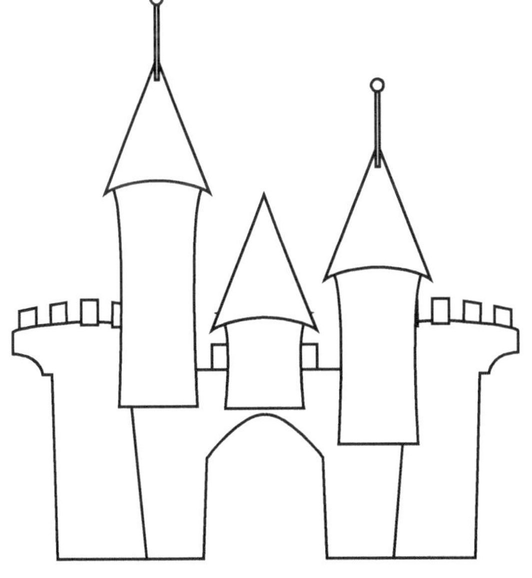

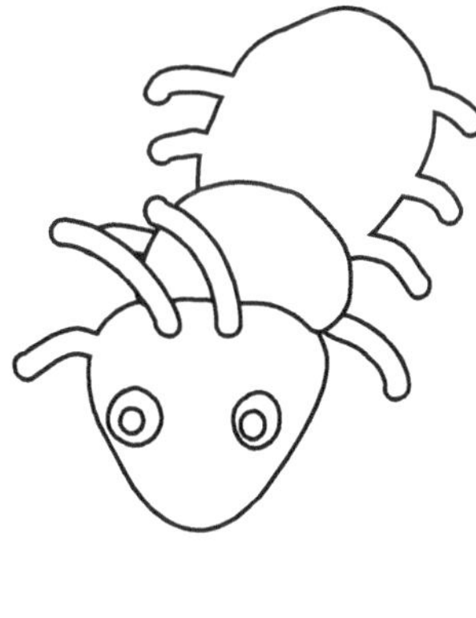

GREEN

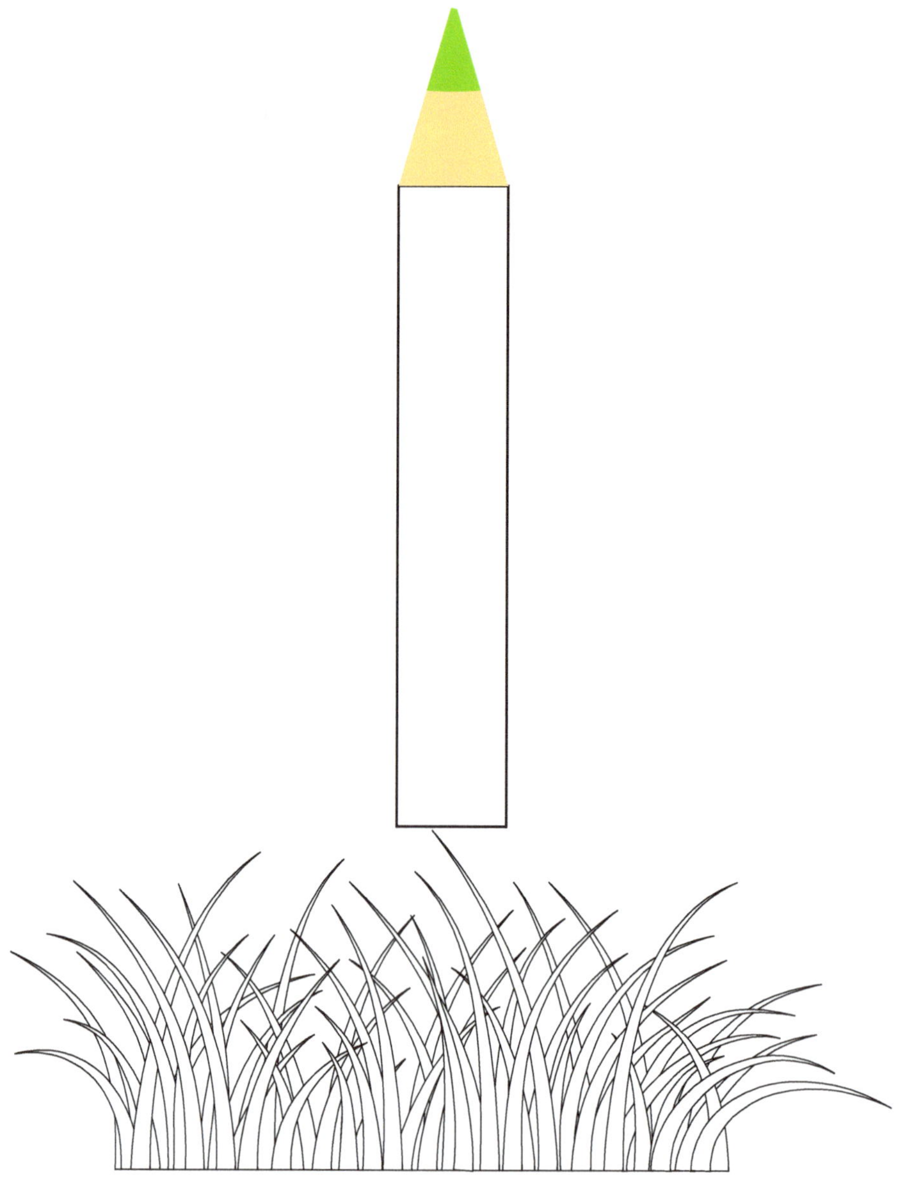

DARK BLUE

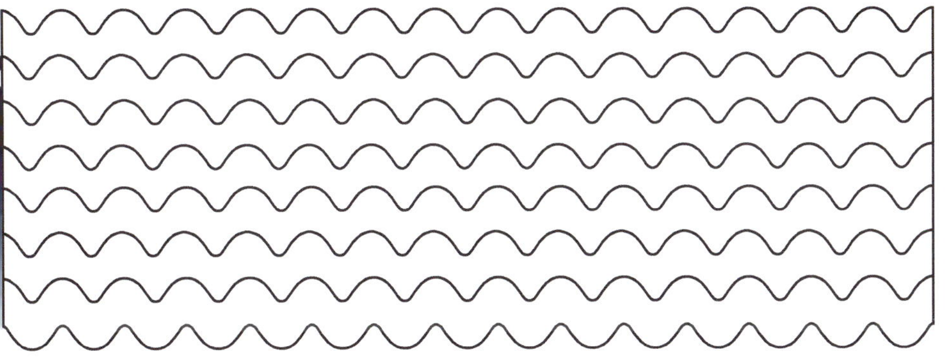

YELLOW

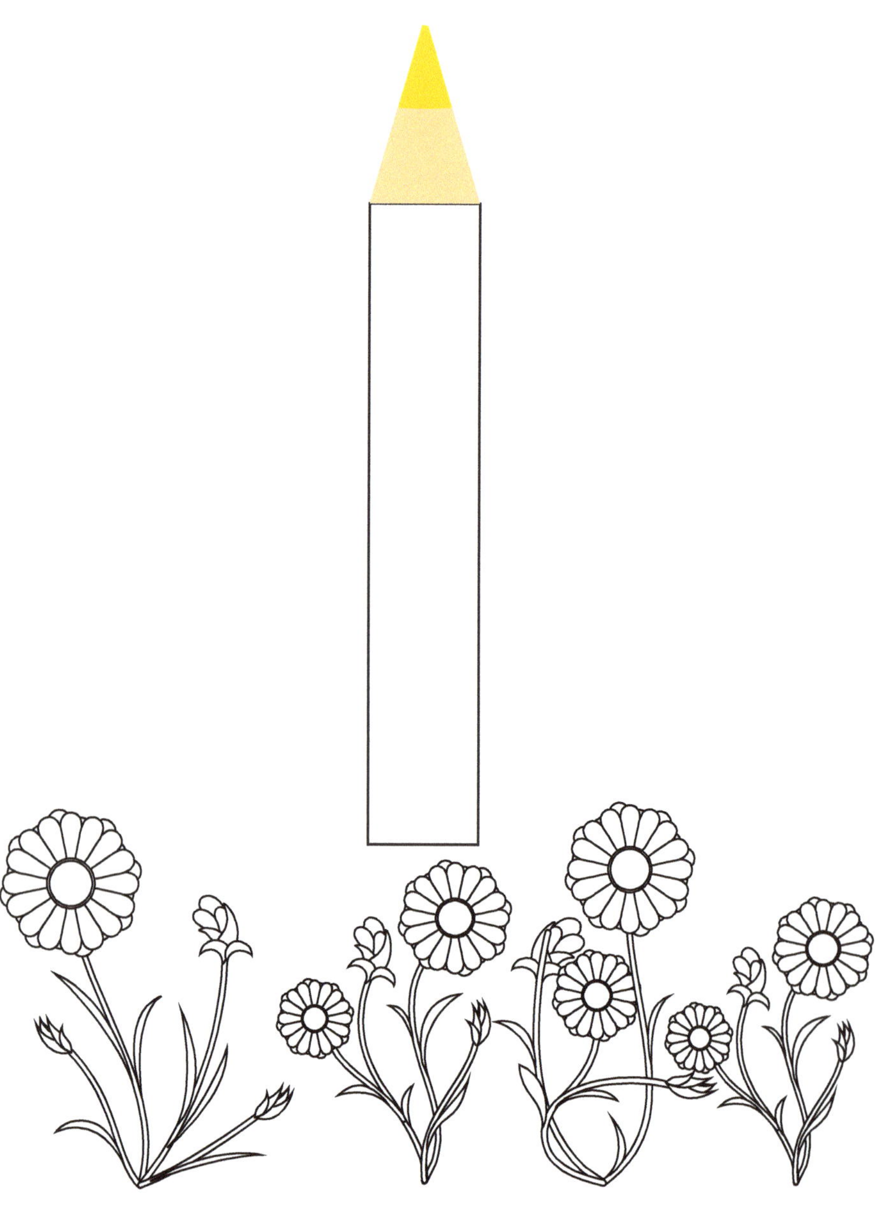

ORANGE

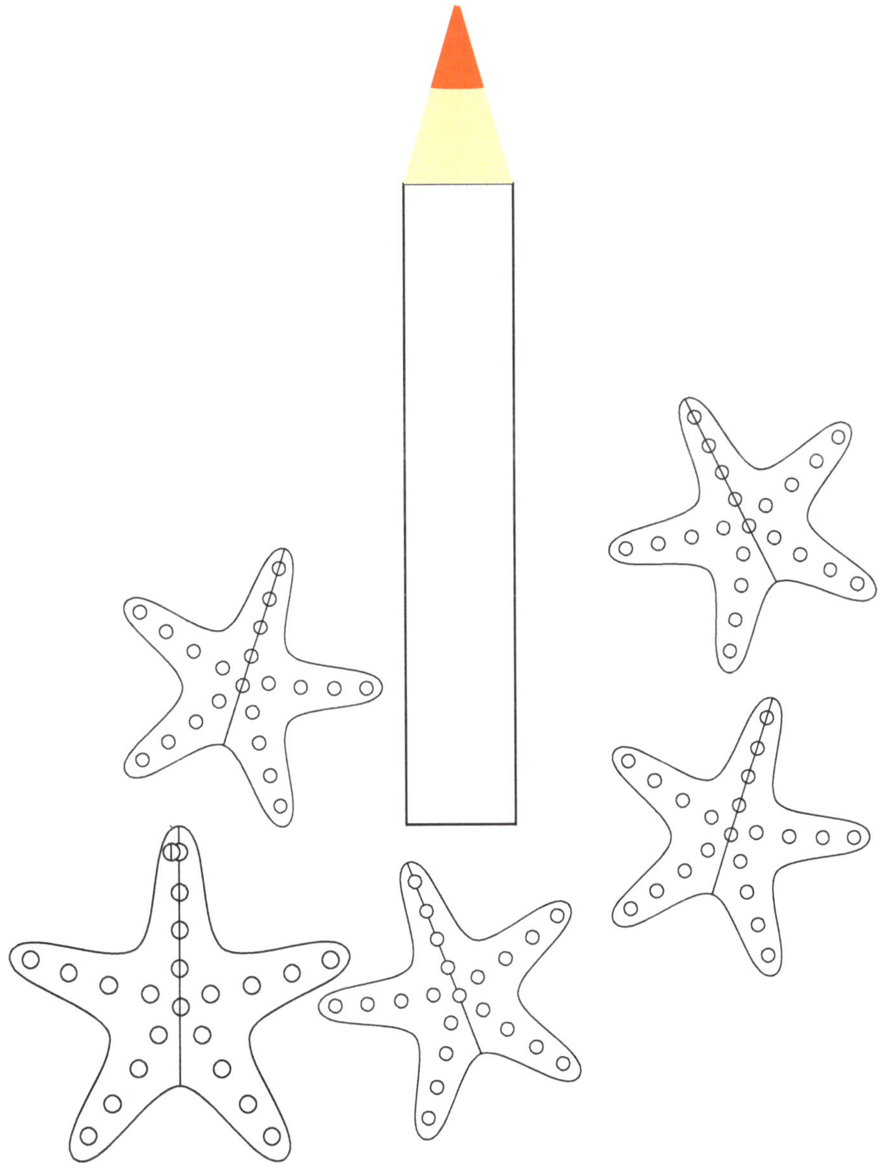

PURPLE

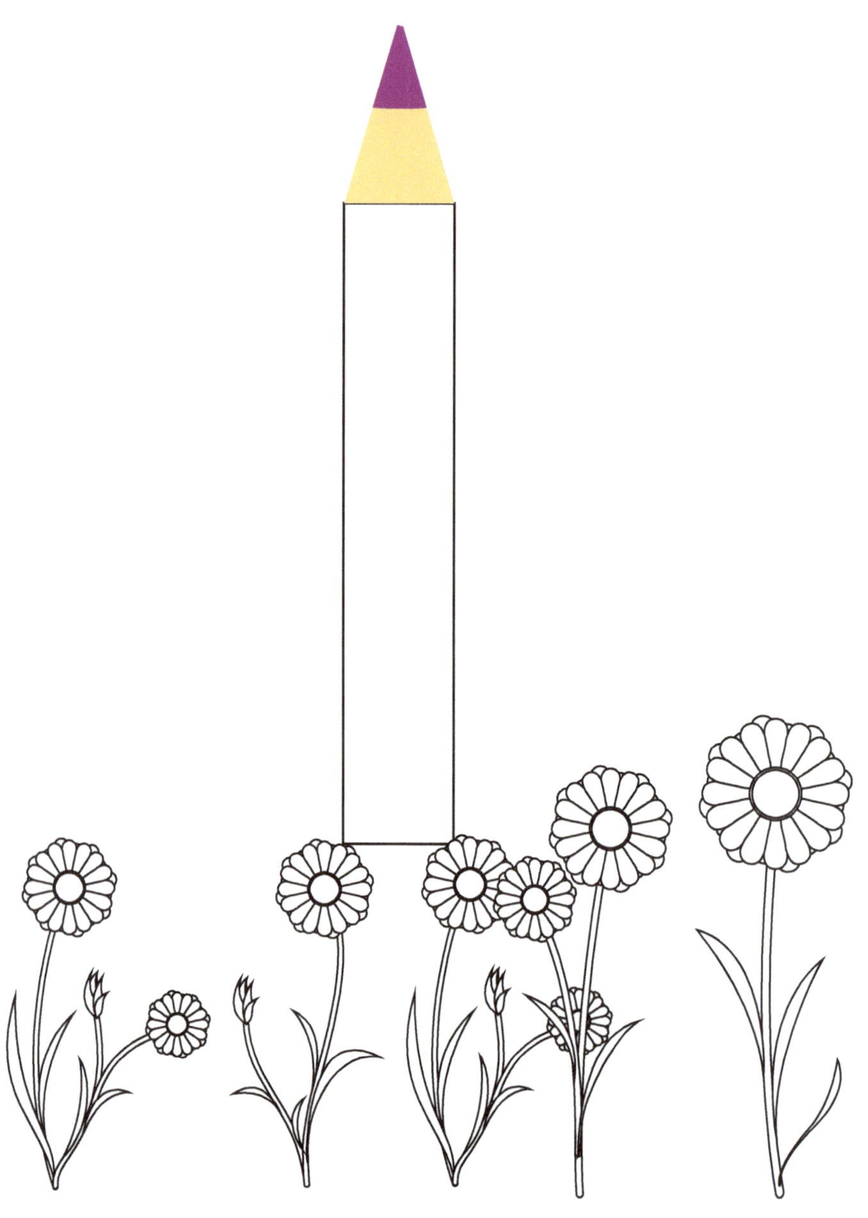

LIGHT BLUE

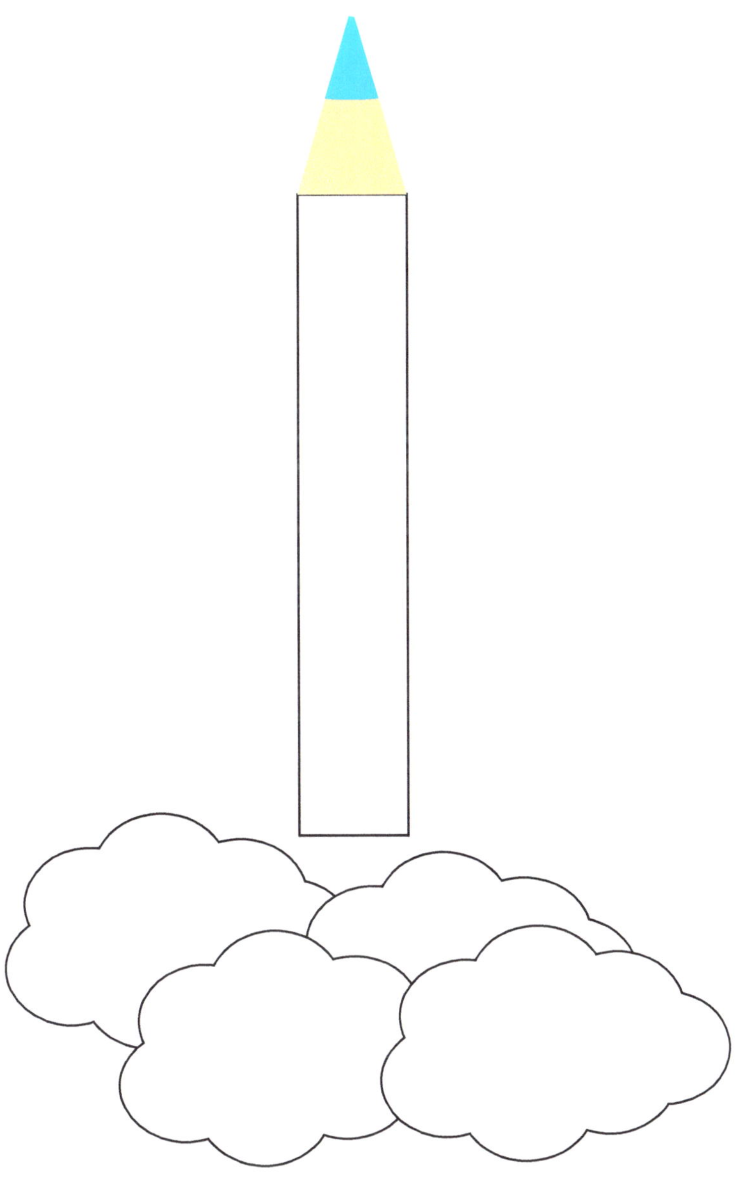

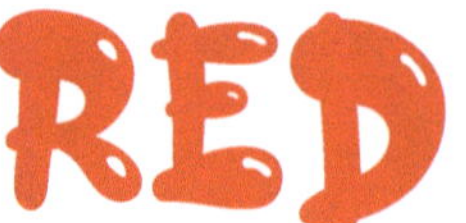

RED

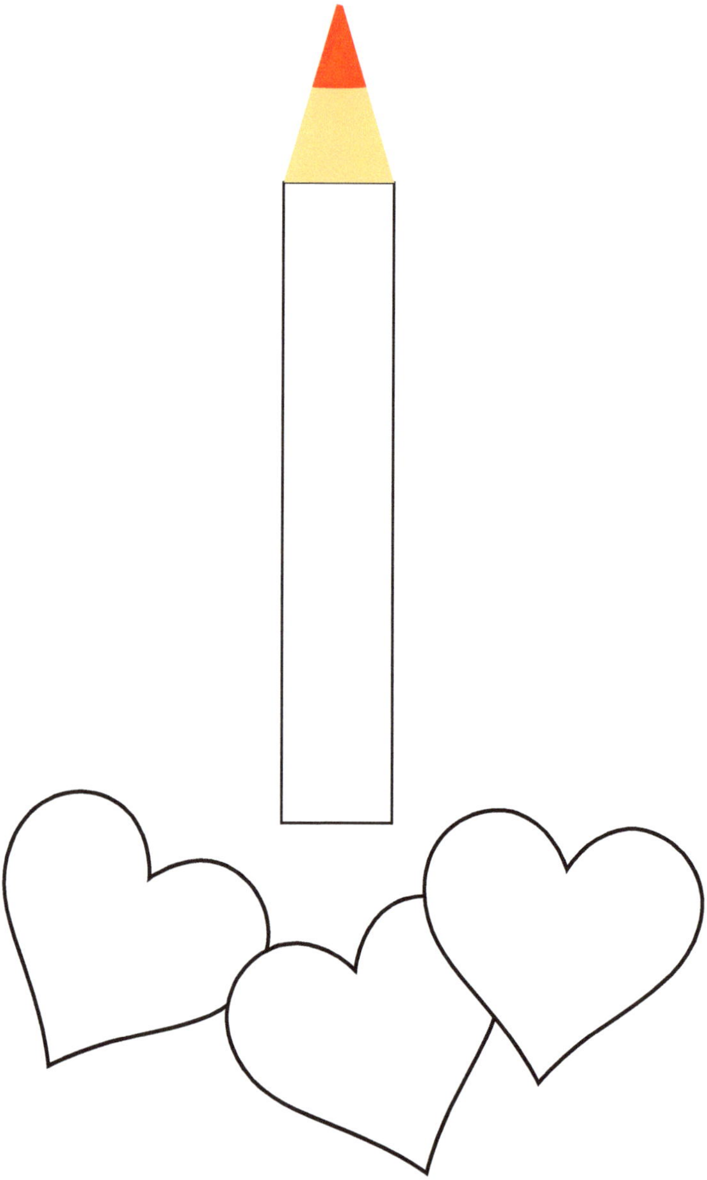

BROWN

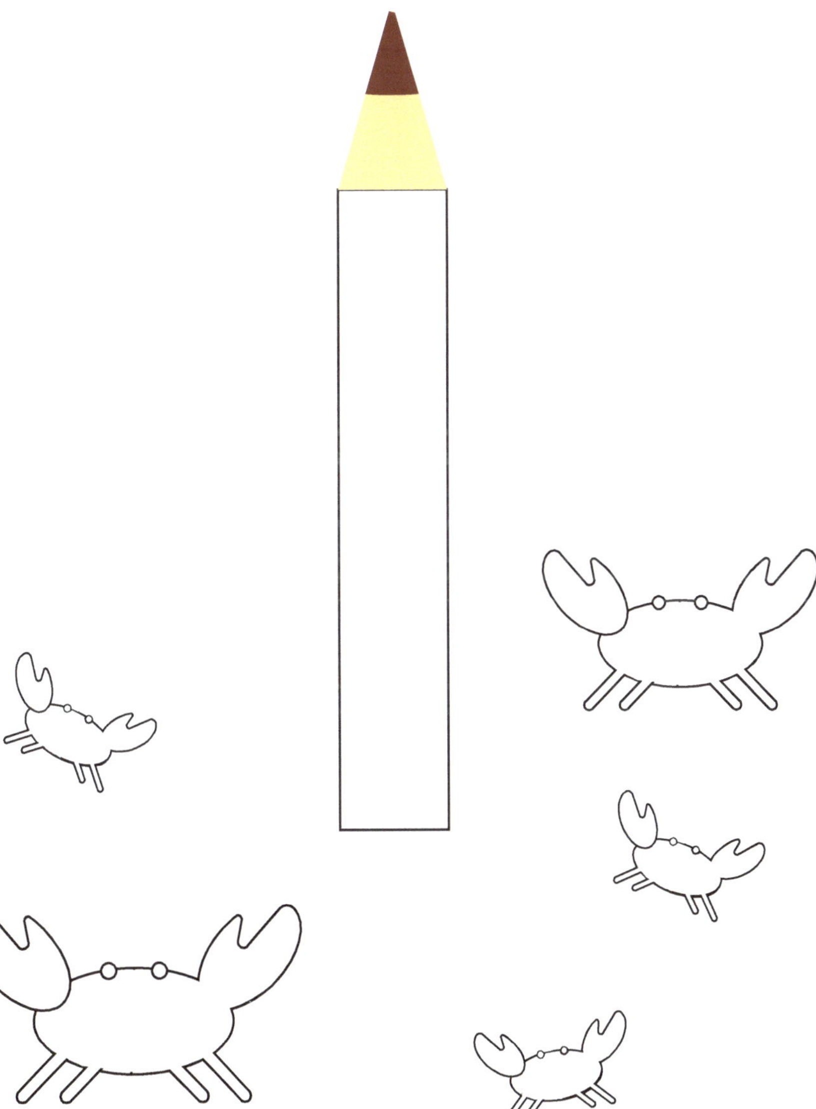

PINK

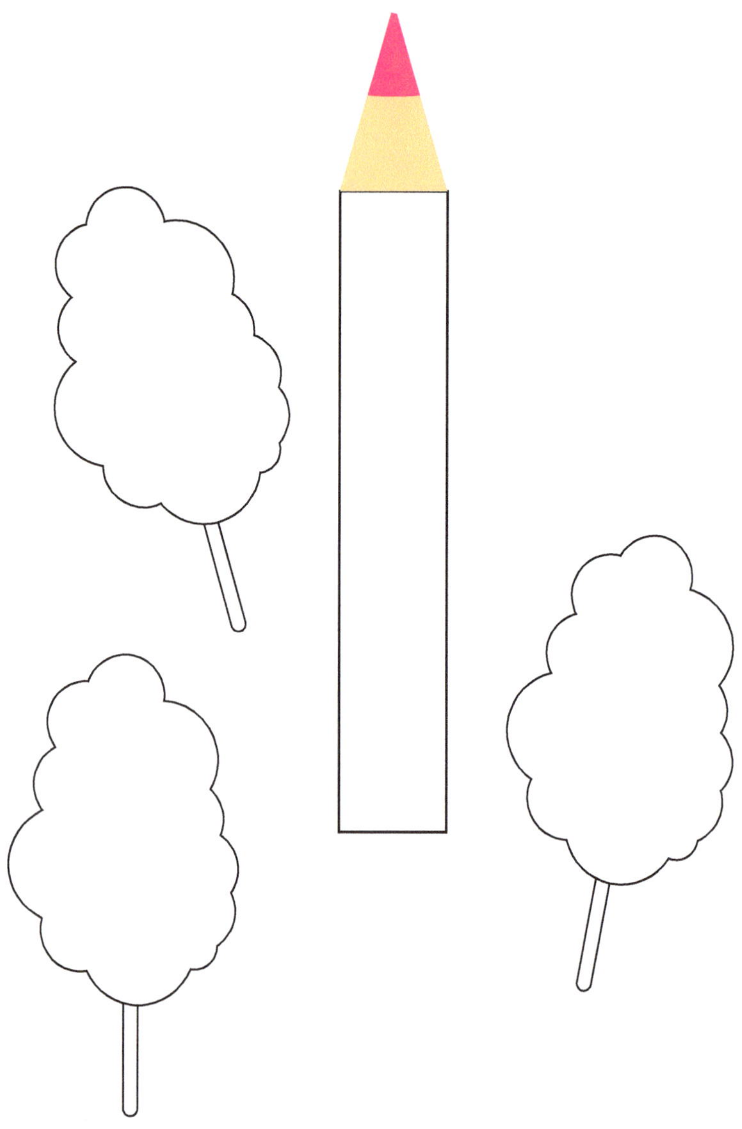

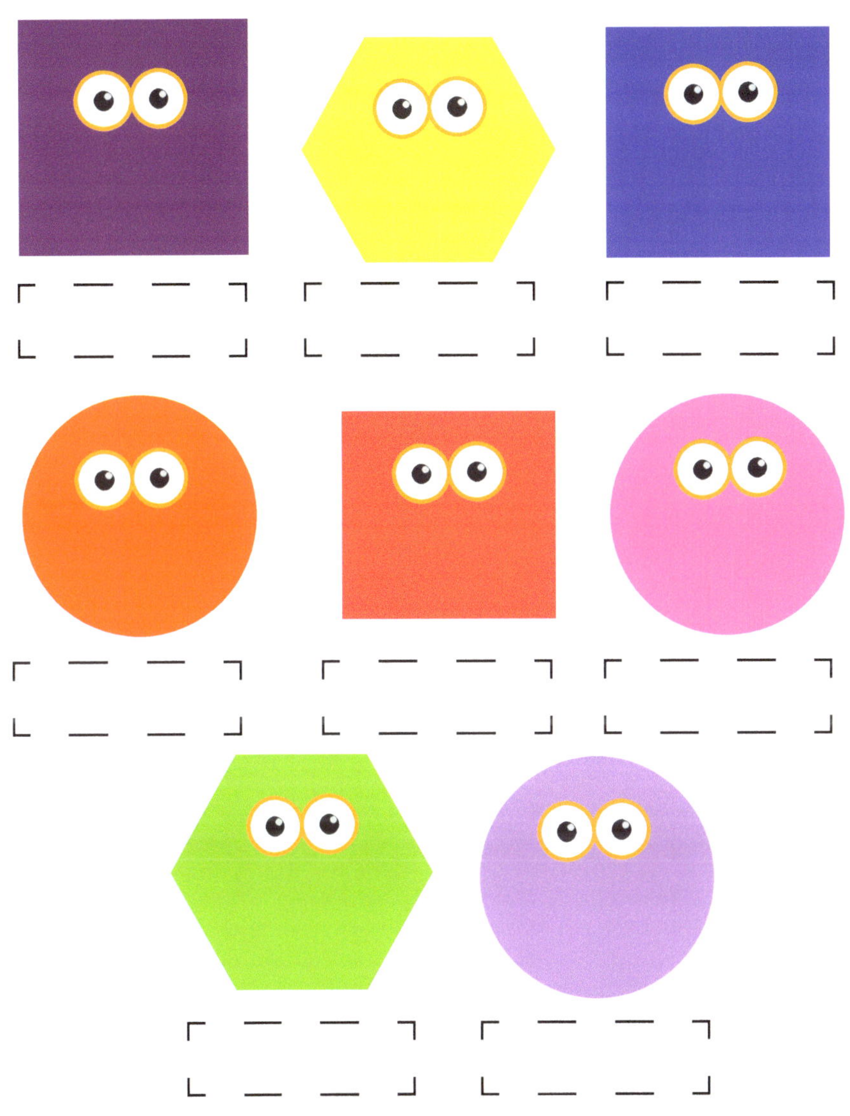

ORANGE PURPLE GREEN PINK
BLUE YELLOW RED VIOLET

Fill colors in the boxes

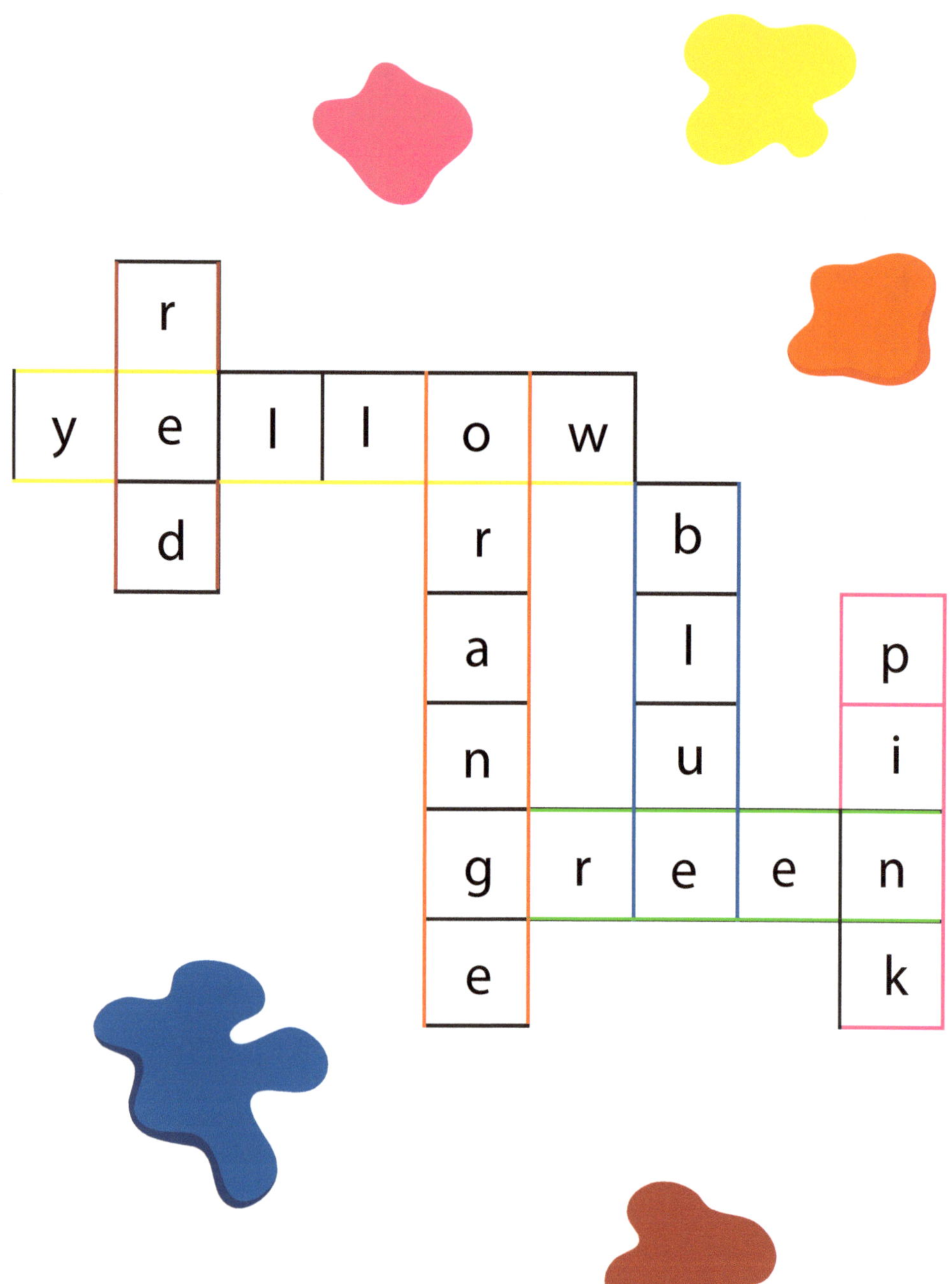

PURPLE

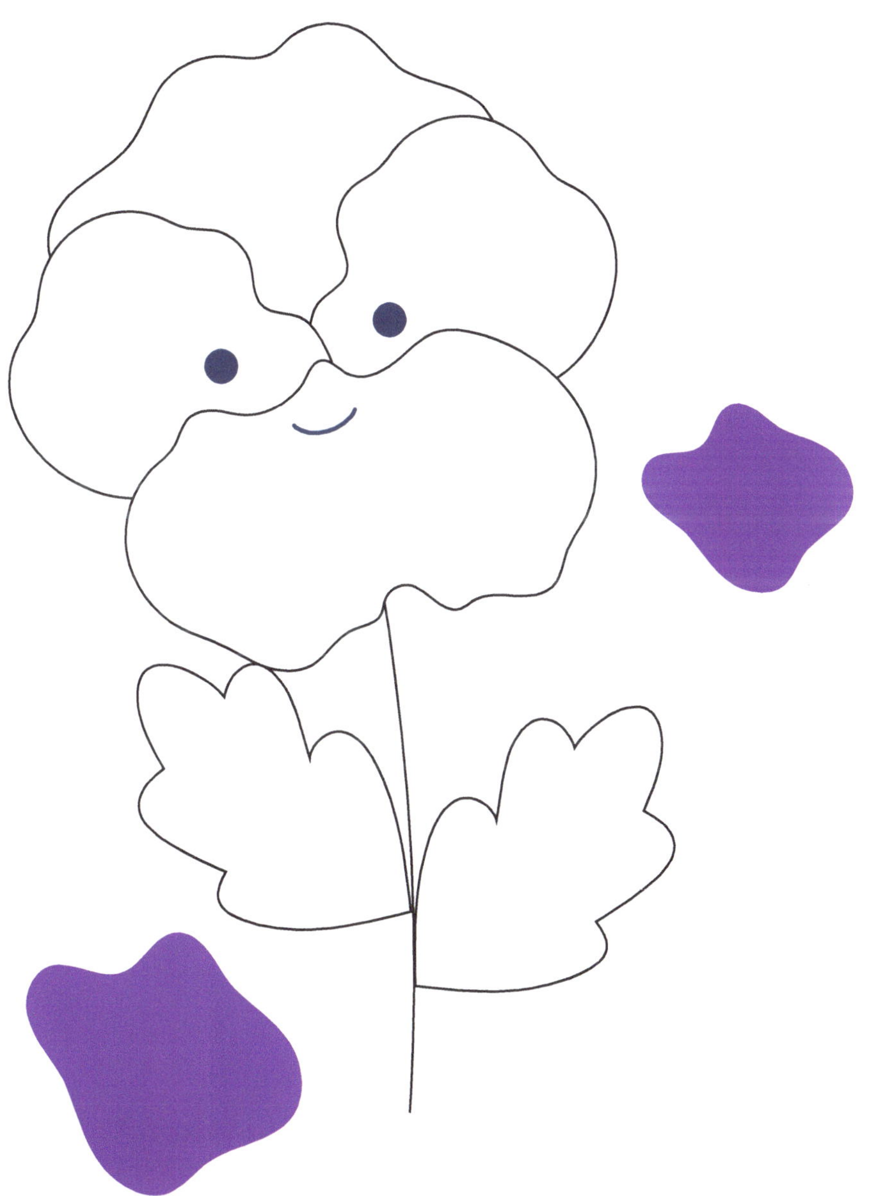

GREEN

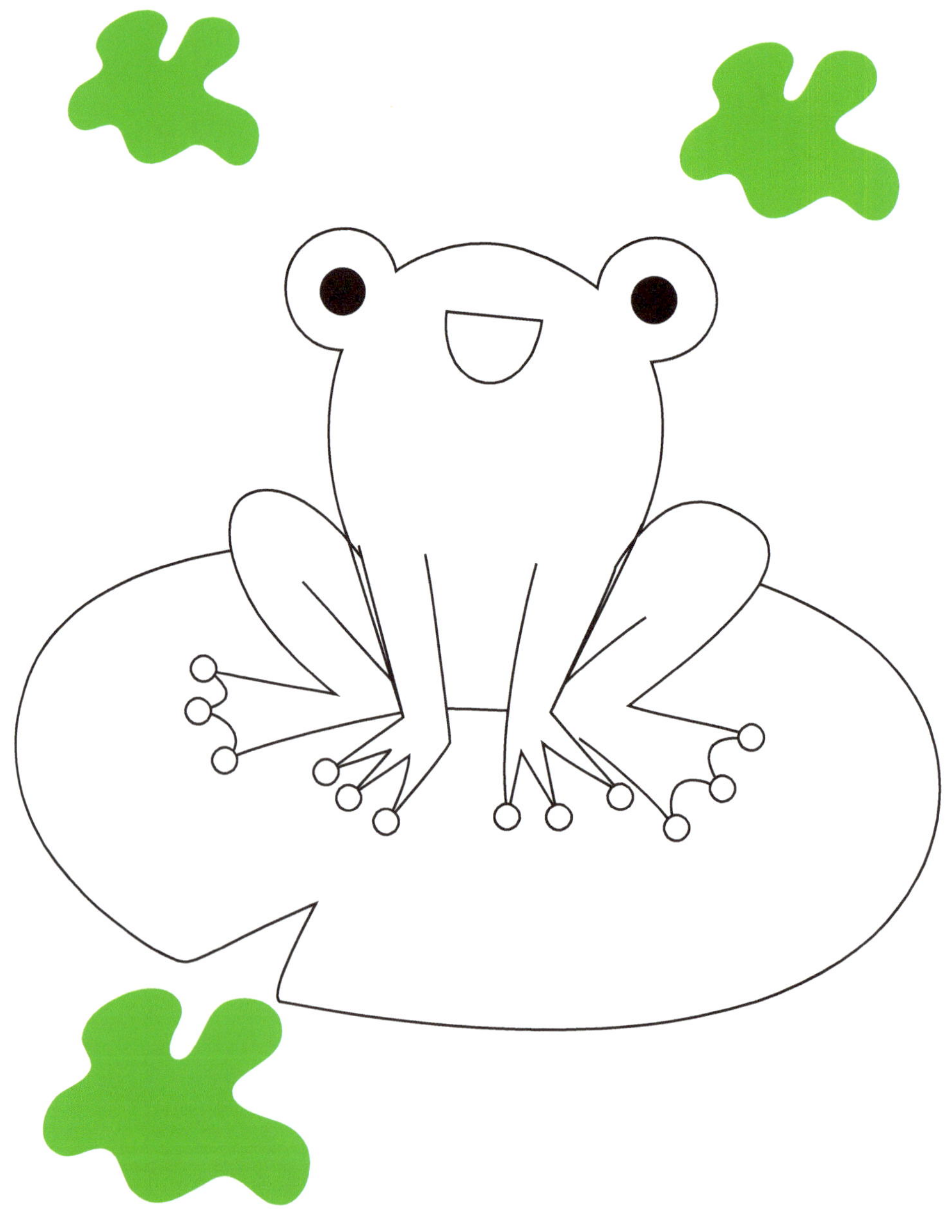

BLUE

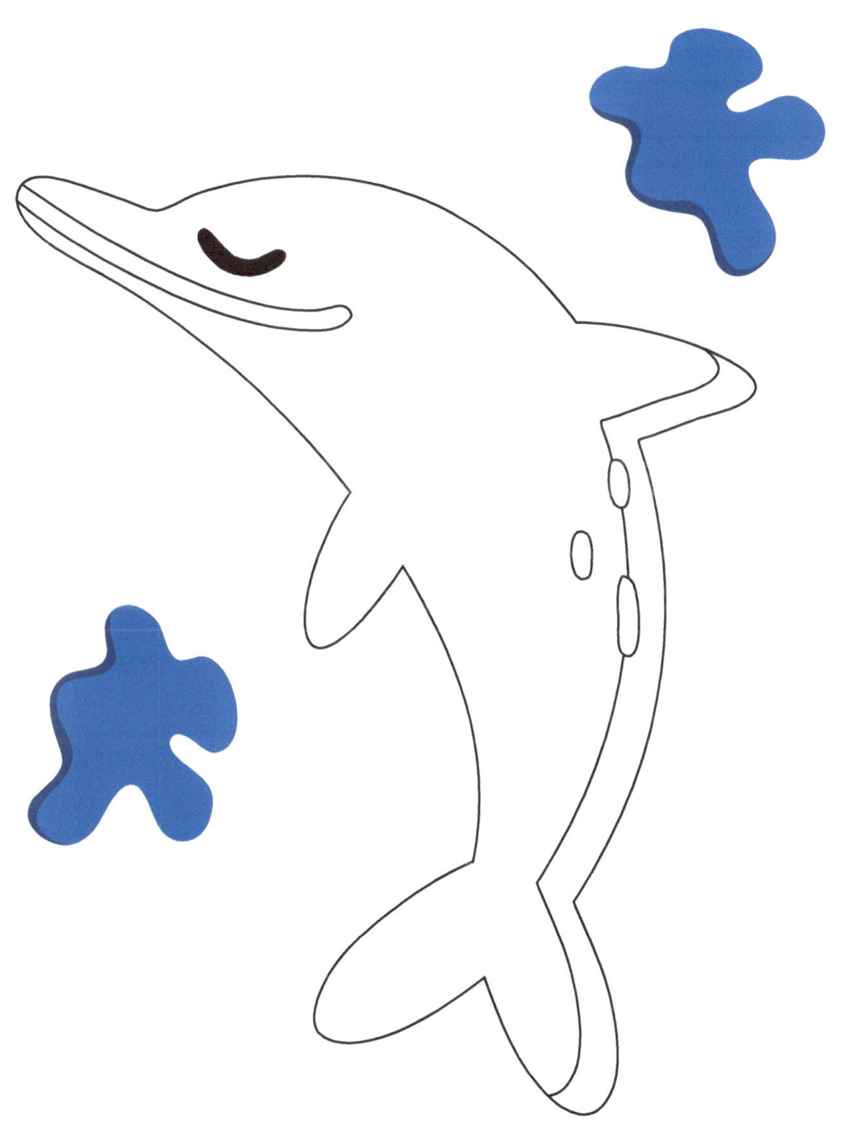

YELLOW

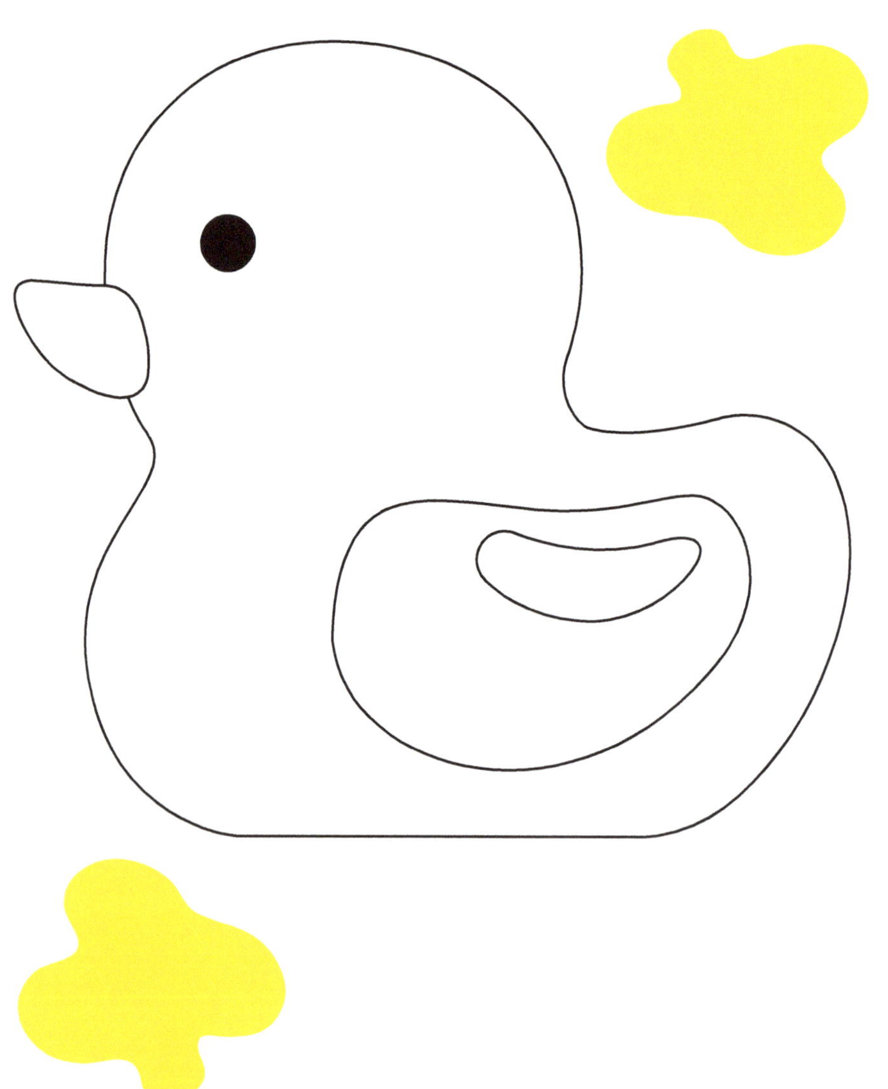

BROWN

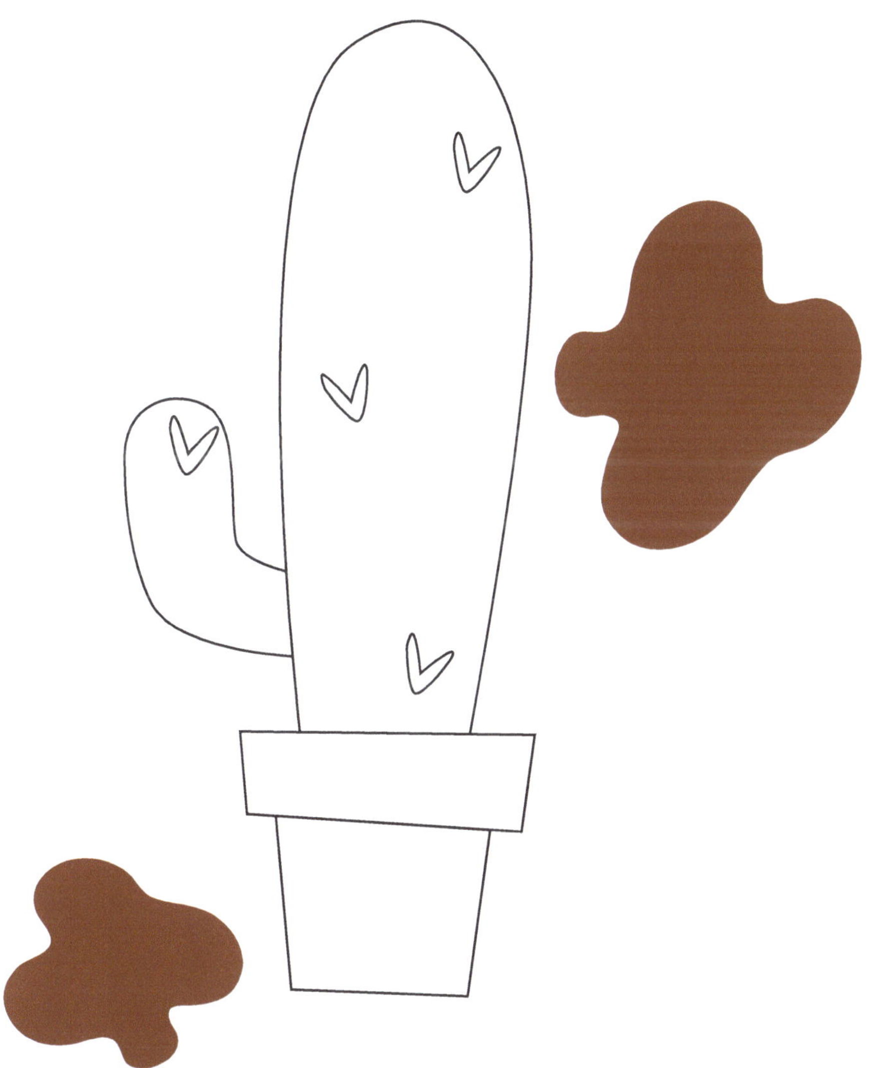

BLACK

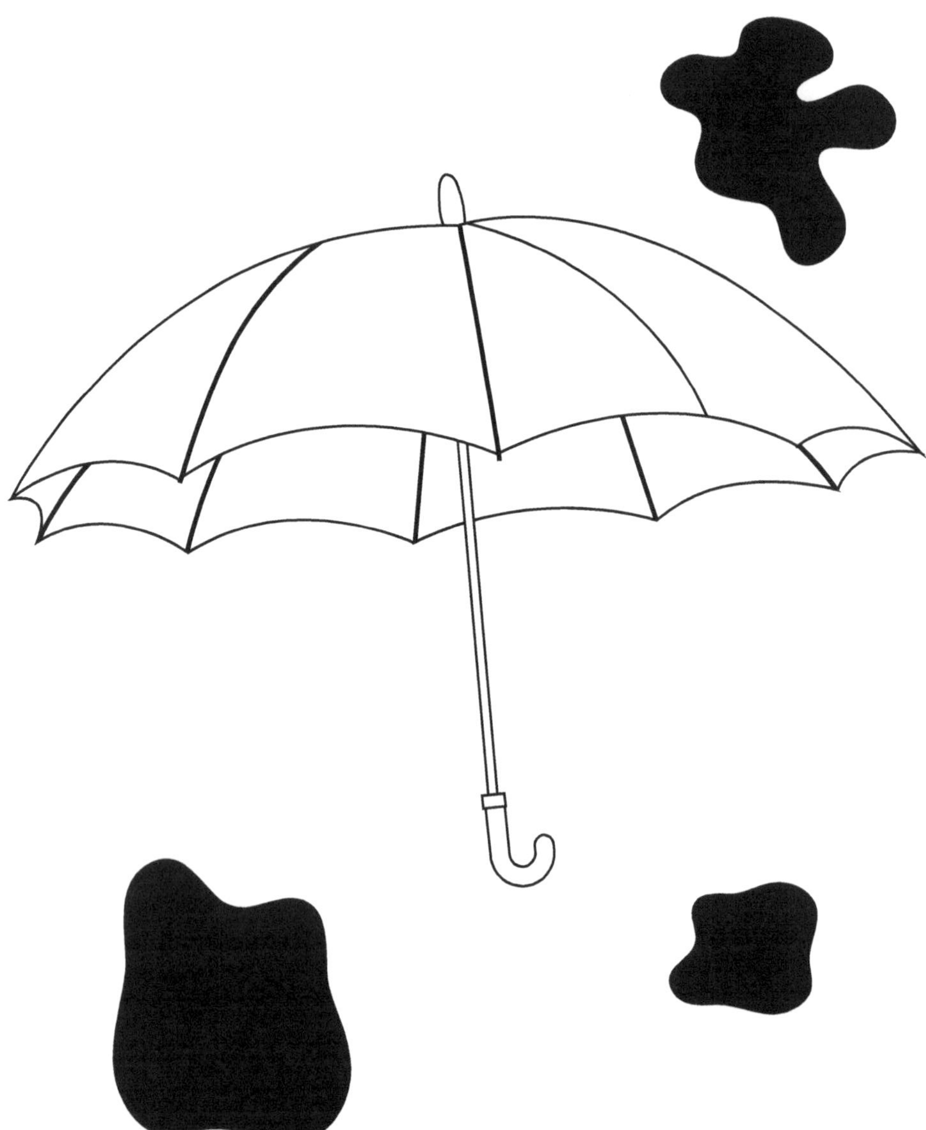

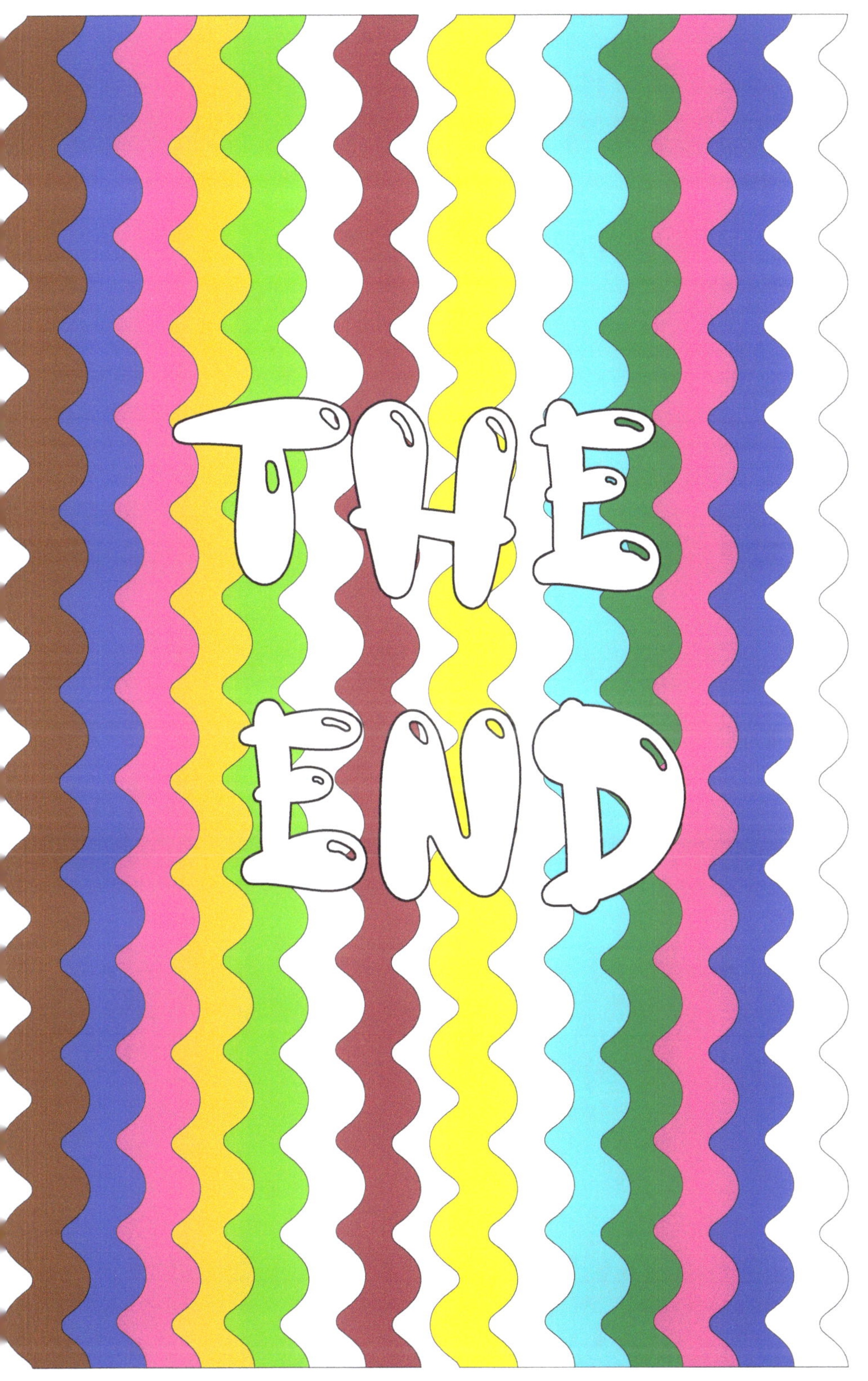
THE
END